Dear Friend: Words of Faith and Life

By: Harold Linginfelter, Jr.

Contents:

Introduction: Why Write Letters

Dear Friend,

I've lived long enough to know life doesn't hand out roadmaps. Most of the time, you just keep walking and figure it out as you go. And along the way, you collect scars, stories, and a few lessons you wish someone had told you sooner.

That's why I started writing these letters. Not because I've got everything figured out, but because I've learned a few things the hard way. If I can hand those truths to you—plain and honest—maybe you won't have to take some of the same hard roads I did.

I'm not writing sermons or speeches here. These are just letters, the kind I'd share across a table or in the shop or on the front porch if we were face to face. Some of them will comfort you. Some might sting a little. But all of them come from a place of wanting you to walk closer with Christ than I did when I was your age.

The next generation doesn't just need advice—they need honesty. They need someone to say, "Here's where I messed up, here's what God taught me, and here's what I'd do different." They need hope that their story can still be rewritten, and a reminder that Jesus never leaves them to walk alone.

So that's what you'll find here. Letters on faith, work, relationships, suffering, hope— pieces of my own journey, mixed with Scripture and truth that doesn't change.

If even one of these words sticks, if it helps you take one step closer to Christ, then it'll all be worth it.

I'm pulling for you.

Harold

A Letter on Faith

Dear Friend,

I didn't always walk in faith. I knew about God, sure, but I leaned more on myself than on Him. I figured if I worked hard, kept control, and didn't stumble too bad, I was doing alright. Truth is, I was just running on my own strength, and it was wearing me down.

Then one day, the Spirit came knocking—but not in the way I expected. It wasn't through a preacher or a church service. It was through a student of mine. Just a young man who saw something in me I didn't even see in myself—the need to pray.

He wasn't trying to be anything special, just stepped up and prayed over me. I don't even remember the words he said, but I remember what happened when I opened my eyes. Something shifted. The weight I'd been carrying, the pride I'd been hiding behind, the empty strength I thought was holding me up—it all broke. A change had taken place. I was different.

That's the thing about faith—it sneaks up on you when you finally stop pretending you've got it all handled. The Spirit will use anybody He wants, even someone the world might call "less important." That day, He used a student to open my eyes. And it reminded me of something I'll tell you plain: be the change you want to see in the world. Don't sit around waiting for someone else to live it first. Step into it yourself. That young man did, and because he did, I couldn't stay the same.

Hebrews 11:6 says, "Without faith it is impossible to please God." I'd read it before, but that day I finally lived it. Faith wasn't about what I knew—it was about who I trusted. And from that moment on, I knew I couldn't keep leaning on myself.

So here's what I want to tell you: don't wait until life knocks you flat to start listening. Tune your ears now. God speaks through people you don't expect, in moments you don't plan. Be willing to hear it. And when He moves, let it change you.

Hold on to Him
—He'll never let go of you.

Harold

A Letter on Identity

Dear Friend,

Identity is a man-given thing. I've carried a lot of titles in my life—teacher, student, leader, follower, hero, even villain. And let me tell you, those titles can weigh heavy. They shape the way you see yourself, and before long, you start bending your life to fit the role somebody else handed you.

The trouble is, titles shift. One day you're celebrated, the next day you're criticized. One season you're the one in charge, the next you're the one learning again. It's hard to live by titles, because they keep changing. And if you're not in Christ, those names become everything. You hang your worth on them, and when the title fades, so does your sense of who you are.

I know that feeling. I've tried to live up to what the world expected, and it wore me out. But when I became a follower of Jesus, all the noise quieted. My title got simple: Saved. No matter what people called me, no matter what role I held, that name stayed.

1 Peter 2:9 says it plain: "But you are a chosen people, a royal priesthood, a holy nation, God's special possession." That's not a temporary badge—it's who you are at the core. And Jesus told us to love one another. As long as you keep that front-and-center, you've already got a good starting point for living out who you are in Him.

So here's the truth I want you to hold on to: the world can take away your titles, but it can't take away your name in Christ. You're His, and that's enough.

Stand tall—you are His.

Harold

A Letter on Integrity

Dear Friend,

Integrity isn't a hard thing to grasp. Do what you say. Say what you do. That's it. Folks make it sound complicated, but it's really not.

I've seen people dance around their words, promising what they never planned to deliver, thinking it sounded nicer than being honest. Truth is, it's easier to hear a straight "no" than to sit waiting for an answer that never comes. Nothing wears down trust faster than empty words.

The Bible says in Matthew 5:37, "Let your 'Yes' be yes, and your 'No,' no." Jesus didn't leave much wiggle room. He knew our words carry weight, and He wanted us to carry them carefully.

Your integrity shows up in the little things. When you show up on time. When you own up to mistakes. When you keep your word even if it costs you. Those small choices add up to a reputation folks can lean on—or one they can't.

So here's my advice: guard your integrity like treasure. Don't spend it cheap trying to impress. If you've got to say no, say it plain. If you give your word, keep it. A man's word ought to be like a good handshake—firm, steady, and binding.

Let your word be solid,
like your faith.

Harold

A Letter on Relationships

Dear Friend,

Relationships are tricky. They don't run smooth on their own—you've got to work at them. And the only way they last is through a mix of compromise, listening, and loving. Not compromise in your faith—never that—but compromise in the small, everyday things that make life livable together.

Sometimes love looks like sitting in a space that makes you uncomfortable just so someone else knows they're not alone. Sometimes it means wading out into the deep waters beside a person who's hurting, even when you don't have the right words. And sometimes love is as simple as showing up in the room, no advice, no speeches—just presence.

The Bible says in Galatians 6:2, "Carry each other's burdens, and in this way you will fulfill the law of Christ." That's the call. Don't let your brothers and sisters drift into isolation. Don't let them slip away quietly. Your call, your visit, your time might be the thing that steadies them, maybe even saves them. If Jesus paid the ultimate

price for salvation, then surely a phone call
or a kind word isn't too much to ask.

So here's what I want you to remember:
real love is often inconvenient, but it's
never wasted. Show up. Listen close. Walk
with people, even when it costs you. That's
the kind of love Jesus told us to have for
one another—and it's the kind that can
change a life.

Don't let folks drift alone
—show up.

Harold

A Letter on Work

Dear Friend,

There was a time when I thought I was the smartest man in the shop. I convinced myself the place couldn't run without me. And once I believed that, I started acting like it—showing up on my own schedule, doing things my way, figuring the company needed me more than I needed it.

Looking back, that was about the worst road I could've taken. It gave my co-workers every reason to dislike me and my employer every reason to cut me loose. Pride will trick you like that—make you think you're untouchable while you're busy digging your own hole.

These days my work looks different. In my current role, I wake up every day filled with the sense that what I'm doing matters in the kingdom of God. And I'll tell you something I've learned along the way—whether you're turning wrenches, teaching a class, or working behind the counter, the job itself doesn't define your worth. What matters is the heart you put into it.

The Bible says in Colossians 3:23, "Whatever you do, work at it with all your heart, as working for the Lord, not for human masters." That means no shortcuts, no half-measures. Whatever task is in front of you, do it with everything you've got. Don't sell yourself short by offering less than your best. Because at the end of the day, it's not about the title— it's about the faithfulness.

Do your work well. Give your all. And when you lay your head down at night, let it be with the peace that you honored God in what you put your hands to.

Do it well, do it for Him.

Harold

A Letter on Failure

Dear Friend,

I've failed more times than I've succeeded. That's just the truth. And every failure left its mark on me. Some scars are still fresh, and some go back decades, but I carry them all the same. They remind me where I've been and what I've learned.

Thing is, I don't run from those scars anymore. I hold tight to them, because each one is a lesson. Without failure, no real success would ever come. You can't build strength without resistance, and you can't learn without stumbling.

The Bible says in Proverbs 24:16, "For though the righteous fall seven times, they rise again." Notice it doesn't say the righteous never fall—it says they rise again. Falling is part of the story, but getting back up is the part that matters.

Don't be ashamed of your failures—they're proof you tried. Don't let them talk you out of stepping forward again. A failure isn't the end; it's just one way of learning how not to do it. Be tenacious. Get up, dust off, and try again. Every scar is a story of grace that carried you further than you thought you could go.

So here's what I'll leave you with: don't fear failure—fear quitting. As long as you rise again, the failure isn't final.

Don't quit—scars are proof you're still moving.

Harold

A Letter on Temptation

Dear Friend,

Before I knew Christ, temptation wasn't really a battle. If I wanted to do something, I just did it. No guilt, no second thoughts. Right and wrong weren't even on the table. But after I became a follower of Christ, things changed. What used to feel normal started to feel heavy, because now I knew better.

Temptation became a new fight—a real one. And I'll tell you this, you can't face it alone. In my case, I had brothers and sisters in Christ who cared enough to walk with me. They listened. They shepherded me. They loved me enough to give me hard truths when I needed them. That kind of fellowship is the guardrail God uses to keep us steady when sin tries to pull us off the road.

But even with people beside you, temptation still knocks. And when it does, I've learned to ask myself one question: "Is this the way I want to spend Christ's blood?" That thought will stop you in your tracks. Because every compromise, every indulgence, every "small" sin was costly—it cost Him His life.

The Bible says in 1 Corinthians 10:13, "No temptation has overtaken you except what is common to mankind. And God is faithful; he will not let you be tempted beyond what you can bear. But when you are tempted, he will also provide a way out so that you can endure it." That verse isn't theory—it's a promise. There's always a way out. You've just got to be willing to take it.

So here's what I'll leave you with: temptation will come. But you don't have to fight it in silence, and you don't have to fall to it either. Lean on conviction. Lean on community. And never forget the price Christ paid for your freedom. His blood is too precious to spend on sin.

Keep fighting the good fight—you're not alone in it.

Harold

A Letter on Money

Dear Friend,

We need money to survive. Can't eat without it, can't keep the lights on, can't drive down the road without filling the tank. I've had seasons where I used money wisely, and I've had times where I squandered thousands. I know both sides.

These days, I rarely even look at bank statements. Not because I'm wealthy—far from it—but because I've come to see money as a tool, nothing more. It gets me where I need to go, puts food on the table, keeps the heat running, and, most importantly, lets me impact the community. The number in the account matters less than what that number is being used for.

The Bible says in Matthew 6:21, "For where your treasure is, there your heart will be also." That verse stings, because it forces you to look at whether your money serves you or serves God's kingdom.

When I die, the bank account won't transfer with me. God isn't going to perform an audit before opening the gates. But He will ask me this: "Were you a good steward of what I gave you?" Don't get it twisted—whatever you've got, it's there because God allowed it. And the question is, how will you use it?

So here's my advice: don't worship money, but don't waste it either. Let every dollar have a purpose bigger than you. Let it serve God's work. Let it bless others. That way, when the account runs out—as it always does—you'll still have treasure stored in heaven where it can't be lost.

Spend it on what lasts.

Harold

A Letter on Suffering

Dear Friend,

I've suffered a lot. I don't tell you that to pull sympathy out of you—I tell you because it's part of who I am today. Truth be told, I'd rather people look at me and see strength instead of scars, but suffering leaves its fingerprints on you. It forces you to look inward, to ask hard questions: Why am I here? What did I do? What am I supposed to learn?

Over time, I've learned how to suffer in solitude. Not because I enjoy it, but because I know I need to feel it. I don't want to be blindsided by pain or numb to the reality of it. If you've got a heart for serving others, you have to know what suffering feels like. You need intimate knowledge of sorrow if you're going to walk alongside people who are carrying it themselves.

Now, I don't mean chasing pain in some masochistic way. But I do mean understanding that sorrow has a place in your walk. There's nothing short of death that can compare to the sacrifice Jesus made for us on that cross. So it's okay to be sad. Look at Job—he was crushed, broken, hurting in every way, and still the Word says he never quit rejoicing.

When you're suffering, remember this: you're being honed. The blade doesn't get sharp without the grind, and the vessel doesn't get strong without the fire. When you make big moves in the kingdom, you'll often face big emotions. Don't run from them. Let God use them.

So if you're in the middle of it right now, hear me—suffering is not wasted. It's shaping you into something greater than you can see right now.

Let the fire shape you, not destroy you.

Harold

A Letter on Calling

Dear Friend,

I'll be straight with you—I don't always know if I'm following my calling the way God intended. I don't have a perfect roadmap. What I do try to do is "feel" the Spirit in whatever I put my hands to and ask, Is this pleasing to Him? That question keeps me steady when I don't have all the answers.

I've had some big personal moments in life —times I was celebrated, times I hit milestones I thought would define me. And while I'm proud of those, they don't even come close to the joy I've felt watching a student of mine do well, succeed, and stand on their own two feet. Nothing beats that. It's a joy that sinks deeper than recognition ever could.

That's what calling feels like—when the thing you're doing fills you with a kind of joy that doesn't wear off quick. Not happiness that fades with applause, but a joy that lingers because you know it mattered.

The Bible says in Ephesians 2:10, "For we are God's handiwork, created in Christ Jesus to do good works, which God prepared in advance for us to do." That means your life has purpose baked into it. And while we may wrestle with the details, God already knows what He built you for.

So here's my advice: don't get paralyzed waiting for a neon sign from heaven. Find the thing that fills you with joy in Christ, the thing that blesses others, and pursue it with everything you've got. If it pleases Him and it builds up His people, you're walking in the right direction.

Chase the joy He planted in you.

Harold

A Letter on Leadership

Dear Friend,

I'll tell you something I wrestle with: church as a business. I understand the need for structure, for systems, for order—you've got to keep the lights on, manage the money, and organize the people. But I've never been able to come to full peace with treating the church like a corporation. And because of that, I've found myself at odds more than once with how things are run behind the scenes.

The thing is, Christ-centered leadership doesn't look like business leadership. It flips the whole idea upside down. Out in the world, leadership is climbing higher, having more control, making more decisions. But in the kingdom, leadership means going lower to lift others higher. Jesus said in Matthew 20:26–28, "Whoever wants to become great among you must be your servant, and whoever wants to be first must be your slave—just as the Son of Man did not come to be served, but to serve, and to give his life as a ransom for many."

That idea of "going lower to go higher" gets lost sometimes. People chase influence but forget servanthood. They want the title but not the towel. Yet Jesus Himself led by washing feet, not by drawing paychecks.

Now don't get me wrong—the church, even with its flaws, is doing great things. Whether or not I agree with every decision behind closed doors, I can't argue with the fruit. Lives are being changed. People are meeting Christ. Hope is being restored. And that's the heart of it.

So here's what I'll leave you with: leadership in Christ's kingdom isn't about position, it's about posture. It's not climbing ladders, it's carrying crosses. If you want to lead, serve. If you want to be great, go low.

Lead by serving—go lower to go higher.

Harold

A Letter on Church

Dear Friend,

Have you ever been told a truth that stopped you in your tracks? A truth so clear, so rooted in Scripture, you couldn't argue with it even if you wanted to? Those kinds of truths are supposed to come from the church body.

The problem is, we sometimes confuse being "nice" with being Christlike. We don't want to ruffle feathers, so we go quiet. But when we sacrifice standards for comfort, we stop helping each other grow. The church should never be cruel, but it also shouldn't be spineless.

The Bible tells us to love one another, but it doesn't say love means letting each other do as we wish. Love means caring enough to speak truth. Love means walking with someone through conviction, not just clapping for them in compromise.

I've learned this: if no one tells you you're doing the wrong thing, how will you ever learn? We need each other to hold us steady. We need the body of Christ to call out sin and call us back to Him—always covered in love, always rooted in the Word, but clear enough to correct.

The Bible says in Proverbs 27:6, "Wounds from a friend can be trusted, but an enemy multiplies kisses." I'd rather a brother wound me with truth than flatter me into destruction. That's what church is for— helping each other grow in Christ, even when it stings.

So don't shy away from truth in the body. Speak it with love, receive it with humility, and trust that God uses both to shape us into who He's calling us to be.

Speak truth with love, and let it grow you.

Harold

A Letter on Hope

Dear Friend,

For most of my life, I had no concept of hope. I was hopeless. Depression colored everything in shades of gray. Add to that the constants of life—death, taxes, grinding away at an occupation—and it was a recipe for ruin.

I hated who I was. I marked my body with tattoos, convincing myself they would "mask" the emptiness inside me. But they didn't. I was just a broken, robotic husk, driven by the carnal desires of the secular world. And in time, I convinced myself that hopelessness was simply my role. Misery was the script, and I had resigned myself to play it out.

But then...

My story isn't dramatic in the way some testimonies are, but it is miraculous. A follower of Christ reached out to me. Just a small act of care, nothing flashy. And when I finally let my guard down and submitted enough to let him in, the Spirit slipped through the cracks I'd been trying so hard to cover.

And in that moment, I felt something I had never felt before—hope. Not optimism, not self-help, not "trying harder." Hope. The kind that runs deeper than feelings. The kind that comes straight from knowing I am God's child. As much as I had given up on myself, God hadn't given up on me. He showed me in a way I could never deny that I had meaning, I had purpose, and I had a future.

Romans 15:13 says, "May the God of hope fill you with all joy and peace as you trust in him, so that you may overflow with hope by the power of the Holy Spirit." That was me—empty, hopeless, until His Spirit filled me up and overflowed what I thought I'd lost forever.

So if you're sitting in that gray place, hear me: you're not stuck. You're not forgotten. You're His child. And in Him, you have meaning, you have purpose, and yes—you have hope.

Look to the Light—hope is yours.

Harold

Conclusion: My Prayer for You

Dear Friend,

I pray that you have the courage to step into the wonderful life Christ has set before you. The journey won't be easy, but you won't walk it alone. Christ walks with you. Your brothers and sisters in Christ walk with you. And when you find yourself in moments of weakness, all you have to do is ask Him for strength. It's laid out plain as day—all you have to do is ask.

I pray you discover the hope and joy I've found in Him. That even if you face dark places, you'll lift your eyes to the Light of the world.

And I pray blessings and protection over you and your family—that His hand will guide your steps, steady your heart, and remind you daily that you belong to Him.

Walk with courage. Walk with Christ.

Harold

A favor from the Author

Thank you for buying and reading this book. Whether it lifted you up, challenged you, or even rubbed you the wrong way, I'd be grateful if you left a review. Your words help others know what to expect and keep these messages moving forward. And if this book spoke to you, I invite you to check out my other works as well. God bless you and your family.

—Harold

Made in the USA
Columbia, SC
25 November 2025

73793775R00020